TWISTS AND TURNS

3 Monologues for Women
3 Monologues for Men

Stephen Baker

Running time for each monologue
10 - 15 minutes

TSL Drama

Rights of performance

Contents

4

Consequences

Lucy is in her early 20s and is a slim attractive brunette. She has struggled since leaving school to hold down employment. She currently works in a massage parlour, as a 'masseur'.

Setting

Scene 1: Staff room massage parlour: Table and chair
Table, bottle of wine, one glass
Clock
Scene 2: Court waiting room: wooden chair
Scene 3: Hostel staff room: Table and chair, mug

Performance time:

10 minutes

Scene 1

Lucy sits in the staff room of the massage parlour. She is dressed in a nurse's uniform. She has a watch hanging from a pocket on her blouse. The room is basic with a television, a kettle and cups. Above Lucy is a clock that shows 7.30 p.m. On the table in front of Lucy there is a bottle of wine and one glass.

Officially, I am on duty now. They like us to start half an hour before a booking. One of my regulars has booked me for 8 p.m. He likes me to dress in a nurse's uniform, and we do a little role play; me pretending to examine him … blah, blah, blah. He likes to think that he has seduced a nurse. Gives him a good feeling. Me? I feel nothing. The arrangement here is the punter pays the receptionist the door money and he gives me the 'extra' if you see what I mean.

Pause.

I expect you are wondering what has brought me here. Well the answer is life I suppose. Life brought me here. I struggled at school and left with very few qualifications. Had a few personal issues, you see. I found work difficult to hold onto. Had various problems with work colleagues. If I had a pound every time I heard the words: 'We're letting you go Lucy,' I'd be a rich woman. Then I wouldn't have to work here.

Pause.

I was down on my luck a few months ago. Between jobs, getting hassle from the benefits people. Then I saw the advertisement for a masseuse at a Gentleman's Club. No experience required, will train. So I rang the number, and spoke to a woman, who basically runs it with her husband. She asked me to come for a chat at the parlour. It wasn't like a normal job interview, bring your CV and two references sort of thing, and dressing formally.

Pause.

I saw Shirley the owner, she works on reception with another lady. Shirley told me what to expect. Her husband came in and he spoke to me on my own. He basically, was looking more than talking. He was putting himself in the punters' shoes. Touching the 'merchandise' at will, basically.

Pause.

I was asked when I could start and what holidays I had booked. The sort of thing you generally get asked when being inter-viewed. I spoke to a couple of the girls when I started my first shift. They'd all had the interview with Shirley and the 'once over' by her husband, or the 'shagability test' as one girl put it.

Pause.

I suppose I was nervous at first, but you soon get used to it. I've had all sorts of men wanting my services, dress like this, do this. But then there's the talkers. They're the worst kind. I'd sooner just get down to it really. I've my own problems to deal with, without listening to someone else's. If I'd wanted to listen to someone's problems, I'd enrol at the local college on a counsel-ling course.

Pause.

And if I hear 'my wife doesn't understand me' once more, I'll scream. And with one bloke it was: 'My husband doesn't under-stand me.' I thought you can say that again darling.

Pause.

(*She looks down at her watch.*) Oh well, must dash, I have a patient to attend to. (*She gets up and walks towards the door.*)

Fades.

Scene 2

Lucy sits in a court waiting room. The sign behind her reads: Hull Magistrates Court, Waiting Room. She is dressed in very smart apparel.

Well here I am after another court appearance. My other offences were mainly shop lifting and resisting arrest, that sort of thing. This one's a bit more serious. I was charged with prostitution.

Pause.

Basically, what happened was the police did a raid on the massage parlour and I, and another girl, got nicked.

Pause.

I was working the next night after I'd seen my regular patient. I was asked to attend this creepy old guy, who wanted me to wear stockings and suspenders, high heels etc. The attire was a bit of a problem when the raid occurred; as I was hardly able to climb out of the window and do a run for it.

Pause.

Apparently, the police had received a tip off that sex was being offered for money. They waited outside in an unmarked van, and when they were satisfied that men were inside they rushed in. Of course, Shirley the owner denied any knowledge of illegal activity. She had very craftily put signs up stating any girls offering anything more than a massage, will be dismissed.

Pause.

When the police barged into my room I was rather busy at work, doing my job, if you see what I mean. Also, had over two hundred pounds in a tin, in a drawer near the bed.

Pause.

I was bang to rights, as they say, if you'd pardon the pun.

Pause.

So me and Nikki are the only ones done. Our clients get a warning. The police send a letter to them at their address, in the hope they are married and have to explain themselves to the missus. We go to court. The owners get nothing because they had prepared for this day, from the off.

Pause.

The judge looked at me in the dock and said, 'There are always consequences for your actions, Lucy.' He looked at my police record and seen that I'd received a custodial sentence for my last offence of shop lifting and hitting a security guard.

Pause.

My brief argued that I was a recovering alcoholic and that I was of good character, but with the occasional lapses. He told the judge that a custodial sentence was not the answer; and asked for community service.

Pause.

Luckily, the judge agreed. It was suggested that I work at a women's hostel for my penance.

Pause.

It turns out that it's the hostel that I went into when I was released from prison the last time. They basically help women who have just come out of prison to see the error of their ways. Get them sorted, re-housed, that sort of thing.

Pause.

When you watch a film, there is always that catharsis moment; when someone's life changes when an event occurs. And in a strange way, I feel that this is my catharsis moment.

Pause.

I feel a real change coming on. (*She gets up and walks towards the door.*)

Fades.

Scene 3

Lucy sits in the women's hostel staff room. It is furnished very basically. She sits at a table. There is a mug on the table. She is dressed casually.

Do you remember when I said that the court appearance and sentence could be my catharsis moment? Well, I think that it was.

Pause.

I was only supposed to do 100 community hours here as my penance. I approached the manager and told her that I was getting so much from working here that I wanted to stay on. 'Oh, that's fantastic, Lucy,' she said.

Pause.

She couldn't hide her enjoyment. She just kept looking at me after that, every time she saw me.

Pause.

The only problem is that the reason I gave for staying on wasn't the real reason. I couldn't tell her that.

Pause.

When I said felt a catharsis moment in the court, I wasn't lying. I just was being a bit economical with the information.

Pause.

Somebody else was in court that day. Another woman. No not Nikki. Someone from my past. Seeing her brought about a release of emotion. And she's the reason I have stayed on here. I have timed it perfectly for when she would be released. She received a one year sentence, and I knew she would be out in eight months for good behaviour.

Pause.

I knew she would arrive here. And she has, she's upstairs in her allocated room, asleep.

Pause.

When we saw each other she didn't recognise me, nor when I showed her to her room, or when I took her up a cup of hot chocolate to help her sleep. I guess, I am just insignificant to her now.

Pause.

Oh, but I remember her. She was my English Literature teacher at school, Miss Burns. My favourite teacher and my favourite subject. (*She smiles.*) I loved literature and poetry; and I loved her lessons. I used to hang around after lessons and talk to her about the books I was reading, the Bronte sisters and Jane Austen. *Wuthering Heights* was my favourite. I was talking to her on one occasion. She said, 'I love that you love reading the Classics.'

Pause.

Then she offered to give me more tuition if I wanted. Of course, I said. Who wouldn't? She gave me her home address and phone number, and told me to ring her when it was convenient. Which I did. I was so excited. She told me not to tell any of my friends, parents or teachers. As she didn't want anyone to know that she was giving extra help to a pupil, as it would be seen as unfair on the other girls if they didn't do as well in the GCSE exams.

Pause.

I travelled down to said house one weekend, armed with all my books, pens and notebooks. The lot really. I just wanted to learn.

Pause.

As soon as I got to the house she offered me a cordial drink. Which I gratefully agreed to.

Pause.

My memory is blurred after drinking the orange. All I remember is waking up naked in her bed.

Pause.

When I went home, I had a terrible sense of guilt and self-loathing. A sense of anger, but I never knew where to position that anger. And I never picked up another book.

Pause.

When I saw her in the waiting room at the court, everything came flooding back. And when anyone has been charged with an offence, everyone including the other defendants get to know the crime. And what was she charged with? Drugging a young female and having sex with her, without consent.

Pause.

The judge was lenient, because it was her first offence, oh, really? And the young victim fell apart in the witness stand, when the defence lawyer got to work on her. She admitted that she wasn't a virgin, as if that mattered, and that she couldn't remember fully what happened. Anyway, basically she got a light sentence.

Pause.

When I said she is asleep upstairs, I mean she really is asleep. Well she will be by now.

Pause.

You see, I slipped something in her drink, just like she did to me, and that young girl. There's a rather nasty drug going around. Lots of the women in jail were on it. It causes convulsions, and if you overdose on it, it kills you.

Pause.

Miss Burns got a full dosage. I'm sure when she realised what was happening she will have pressed the buzzer to raise the alarm. Unfortunately, the batteries have been removed. I'll give it another hour, just before I go off shift, then I'll replace them.

Pause.

The next shift will come on after I've gone home. They'll find her. Just another casualty of the drug culture in our jails.

Pause.

As the judge said to me: 'There are always consequences for your actions.' Indeed there are.

Fades.

Dear Prudence

You have to speculate to accumulate

Prudence is 38 and has one sister, Beverley, who is a year older. Prudence is a high flyer and currently is an executive for a large company in the City of London, she is the only woman on the board. She lives alone in a luxury flat on Canary Wharf.

Setting

Scene 1: Boardroom
Scene 2: Lounge armchair, posh flat
Scene 3: Lounge armchair, family house
Scene 4: Bed with window, for sale sign outside.

Performance time:

10 minutes

Scene 1

Lights up.

The song Dear Prudence is played.

Prudence sits alone in the boardroom of the organisation. She is dressed smartly in female business attire.

This is where I belong. Where I was destined to end up. I've always been the one with the drive in the family. Even though I am the youngest, it was me who had determination to succeed. I showed leadership skills practically from the day I was born. Much to the annoyance of my older sister. And I stress my older sister.

Pause.

When we were three and four, Mother asked us both what we wanted from Father Christmas. Beverley said she wanted a school desk and chair. I said I wanted a blackboard. That was because I saw myself as a teacher, Beverley saw herself as a pupil. Subtle difference in attitude and belief.

Pause.

That's how it's been all the way through our lives. Me with the drive and ambition and Beverley settling for second best. When we were at school together, I was the head girl and captain of both the hockey and the netball team. Beverley couldn't even get in either team. Oh she tried, but failed I'm afraid. Shame that.

Pause.

But when you accept second best, that's what happens. Beverley just scraped into university. And because of average grades, ended up at some red brick university up north somewhere. Oh what joy that was for mother and father travelling half way up the country to see their eldest daughter in some God forsaken place. Studying History of all subjects. Comes out of it at the end of the three years with a Desmond. That's right a 2.2. Hardly worth the bother really.

Pause.

I was one of 11 students from the 6th form that went to Oxbridge. The Oxbridge 11 they called us. Posters all over the school naming us all. I was accepted at Oxford to read the Classics. Came out with a Geoff Hurst, that's a First, by the way. I was also president of countless societies. I can't even remember all of them.

Pause.

And if Beverley hadn't embarrassed the family enough. She took up with someone at the university. Not another student. He was only a grounds man. Wow, what a catch! Anyway, he got her in the family way and they end up having a shotgun wedding. She was six months' pregnant when she walked down the aisle. I didn't know where to look.

Pause.

And now she is the mother of three boys. What a gene pool that is, a 2.2 graduate and a grounds man. Oh, sorry he is now a maintenance guy with a white van. Drives around fixing things. The kids are ungrateful little brats. I've stopped buying the eldest two birthday and Christmas presents as they didn't have the good manners to ring their auntie up to thank her for going to the trouble of buying them a present. I expect the youngest will go the same way. When we were younger we were told to stay in when an uncle and auntie were visiting so we could personally thank them for our present. You would have thought that Beverley would remember that. Obviously, she has chosen to forget.

Pause.

Mind you, I didn't go out much. I was too busy doing things in the house. And when aunties and uncles came round it was a great excuse to get the Monopoly game out. I always won of course. Right up my street, that game. Buying property and penalising people for not complying with rules. An absolute dream for a Capitalist like me. Whilst we all played that, Beverley would be outside playing hopscotch or something.

Pause.

Then there would always be the knock at the door from someone at school, asking if I was coming out to play. No, I always said. Father would always sing the lyrics from the Beatles song, *Dear Prudence*. I preferred the version by Sioux and the Banshees. I always liked to think that it was penned with me in mind; even though it was written about 13 years before I was born.

Pause.

I was just always determined to succeed. Even as a child I was planning my life. Revising for exams. She has a pointless degree and is a flower arranger. Works on weddings and things. Well, what ambition she's had. Marries a 'Mr Fixer,' has three kids, two of them ungrateful, and arranges flowers for a living. I could do that blindfolded.

Pause.

And here I am the only woman on the board at Powers and Saunders Property Specialists. And at the meeting that I have just attended, I have been given the task of expanding the property portfolio of the company in London. Other executives unfortunately drew the short straw, someone getting the North and Ed from Cambridge getting Wales! Good luck with that one Ed. This marks the end of austerity and the start of something big. I'm starting straight away. I can't wait to get my teeth stuck into this. It's time for Prudence to come out to play.

Pause.

London is going to be my own personal plaything. I'm going to make this company millions.

Pause.

It'll be like playing Monopoly again. (*She gets up and walks towards the door.*)

Fade out.

Scene 2

Lights up.

Prudence sits in an armchair in the lounge of her apartment. She is dressed smartly and looks immaculate, her hair and makeup make her look stunning.

You have to speculate to accumulate. Which is something that I have always believed to be true. It's a saying you just don't hear now. Austerity seemed to turn everything on its head. The best decade by far for someone like me was the 1980s, when some people could be obscenely rich from property deals. Whilst I was whipping family members at Monopoly, some people were playing it for real. Well now, I'm joining the party. It's going to be champagne most evenings for this yuppie.

Pause.

I've already started on the property portfolio expansion. As soon as my appointment was made Douglas Evans-Deich from my days at Oxford got in touch. He's now one of the main players in the property market. His company is turning over a million a year, and he's responsible for that.

Pause.

Anyway, he got in touch and invited me for lunch at a swanky restaurant in the West End. This is how business is done now, over lunch. So it was a working lunch. Anyway, we got down to business. He said, 'Even though we are working for rival companies, doesn't mean we can't help each other.' Go on, I said. 'Well,' he said, 'I have a chap on the inside of the Council and in the East End there are thirty houses in a particular street, all vacant, and according to my source will shoot up in value soon because of a major development.' What's the development? I said. 'A hotel and a retail store. Top market,' he said. 'Can't say too much more, got to protect my source, you understand.' So, I said why can't your company purchase? He said, 'We've invested heavily elsewhere, and the shareholders are getting itchy feet. However, if you invested, then that would satisfy the shareholders to move into the East End. It's a win, win really.'

Pause.

This was just what I'd been waiting for. A chance to make my mark. Douglas even gave me the contact details of the company who owned the properties. I contacted them straight away. And they agreed to sell after some hard bargaining. All thirty properties for £1,000,000.

Pause.

When I got back to the office there was some disquiet. Protocol and all that. One guy started going on about 'balance and checks' or something. I sort of switched off after two minutes. I reminded everyone that I had been given the authority from the managing director, no less to expand the portfolio of properties. And basically what I say goes.

Pause.

I can be very firm, when I need to be. About two hours later the job was done. We were the proud owners of a row of thirty houses in an area going to be developed with retail and a hotel.

All we need to do is sit tight and wait for the properties to go through the roof, value wise. And I'll be popping the champagne corks.

Pause.

But just to bring me down to earth, mother rang and asked if I would go and see Beverley and the family, bore, bore.

Pause.

I agreed to go on the weekend just to keep mother happy. Never been keen on visiting 'up north' to be blunt. I'm rather fond of my hub caps and I can't understand a word northerners say.

Pause.

Oh well, better get off home and pack for my trip to bandit country. (*She gets up and walks to the door.*)

Fades.

Scene 3

Lights up.

Prudence sits in an armchair at her sister's house.

Lights up.

Well I made it, and up till now the wheel hubs remain intact. This place has never changed in all the time they have lived here. As you walk in the front door you are met with ghastly wallpaper and Beverley's graduation certificate. It's like she is saying this is the only achievement in my life. A 2.2 grade degree.

Pause.

But then we know who was blessed with the drive and ambition in the family.

Pause.

Hubby Tom was pretty useless at conversation. But then I suppose, what would you expect from someone who worked in the grounds of a university and now drives a white van for a living. I mean, he's not exactly the sharpest tool in the box. Hardly going to enter into a discussion about the stock exchange or the resurgence of the property market. No, we kept it simple, we talked about what English people in such situations always talk about – the weather.

Pause.

They'd made some sort of effort to entertain me. Beverley cooked an average meal and Tom had obviously run off to the local supermarket and got a cheap bottle of wine to mark the occasion. Just not what I'm used to I'm afraid. When I buy wine it's a minimum of £250.00 a bottle and I get it from proper wine shops, not the local supermarket. But needs must, I'm afraid, I drank a couple of glasses.

Pause.

I just couldn't stop thinking about my acquisitions, which were done with speed on the accelerated process. All done and dusted in a day.

Pause.

I was just going through the motions with Beverley and Tom. They tried, but all I could think about was work and the achievements I want in the next year or so. I am just so ambitious and I find that because Beverley and Tom are not, I have very little in common with them.

Pause.

It's a shame when you have to say that about your own flesh and blood. But me and Beverley are just poles apart. It's hard to believe that we have the same parents. Well I think we have. We do look similar, but that's where the similarities end really.

Pause.

Beverley chose the marriage and family route and I chose the career. I don't think the two mix personally. I never saw myself changing dirty nappies and cleaning sick off my new Gucci dress. I can put up with my three nephews, but I'm afraid motherhood's not for me.

Pause.

And as for living up north. No thank you. I wonder how many corner shops you need in an area, and where do you do your clothes' shopping?

Pause.

I know one thing for certain, I'll be checking my car before I retire to bed. Car alarm or no car alarm.

She gets up and walks to the door.

Fades out.

Scene 4

Prudence sits alone in her own bedroom at her luxury flat. A for sale sign can be seen out of a window. She is dressed in casual attire and has no makeup on and her hair is tidy but not immaculate. Two large suitcases can be seen on a table.

I expect you're wondering about the suitcases. No I am not going on holiday. I am going back up north. This time for an unspecified time. Beverley and Tom are letting me stay at their place until I find somewhere permanent to live.

Pause.

I am waiting for a taxi to take me to the train station and as you can see the flat is up for sale. Things went a little south as the saying goes. I have had to sell everything I own in order to keep the wolves from the door.

Pause.

When I got back from Beverley's and Tom's about three weeks ago, I was full of the joys of Spring. I had clinched a deal that I believed was going to be the making of me. I expected to be popping corks, not clearing my desk, as I was told to do.

Pause.

Everything was going well until the managing director, Maurice Johnson, called me into his office. When I got there, I was told to sit. There was a long pause, as he sat looking at me. Then he said, 'Do you know the East End of London? Prudence.' Yes, I responded. 'Well obviously, not well enough,' came the response and he added, 'You have just bought thirty properties in a clearance area, that are worthless. The Council will come along shortly and make an offer to this company, which will be market value. Basically next to nothing, given that they are derelict.'

Pause.

I was just speechless. If that wasn't enough, he then really stuck the knife in, if I wasn't already reeling. He said, 'You were seen wining and dining with a member of staff from our greatest rivals, who just by chance have made the real deal in the area. They bought up a street of houses in the adjacent borough, where a retail park and hotel are going be built. I am guessing you were given duff information to throw you off the scent. You've been done up like a kipper.'

Pause.

I was speechless. He looked at me with sternly and said, 'You're fired Prudence. Clear your desk.'

Pause.

Thirty minutes later I was heading out of the door with all my belongings in a cardboard box.

Pause.

I now have no job, and no income. When I got home, I did something I never imagined I would. I rang Beverley and told her what had happened. She offered there and then for me to come and stay with them.

Pause.

Maybe, when we were children, Beverley had the right idea. She was mixing with other children, developing her people skills. Maybe if I had followed suite, I wouldn't have made such a fool of myself, and lost everything.

Pause.

A car horn is heard.

Well, I must dash. I have a lot of catching up to do. (*She gets up from the chair.*)

Fades.

Dizzy Blonde

Kim is an attractive blonde woman in her early thirties. She lives on her own. After coming out of a relationship a year ago, she is ready to find love. She has just started a new job at a call centre.

Setting

Scene 1 and 5: Armchair
Scene 2 and 4: Wooden stool, clock
Scene 3: Kitchen chair and table

Performance time:

12 minutes

Scene 1

Kim sits at home in an armchair. She is casually dressed.

Lights up.

A whole year I've been on my own since I broke up with Ben. It was really not working and I decided that I didn't want him in my life anymore. Very unreliable, is how I would describe Ben. Never where I wanted him to be. And late, he couldn't be on time if his life depended on it. I have very high standards. Don't like scruffiness, he wasn't scruffy, but then he wasn't 'Mr Cool and Trendy' either. He was somewhere in between, if you see what I mean.

Pause.

Anyway, that's in the past. It's all about the future, and I'm looking for Mr Right. I've tried Internet dating but with little success. I don't know why men have such a problem with size. I'm not talking about downstairs. I stipulated in my profile that I wanted someone 5 feet 10 inches plus. I would have thought that's not being ambiguous. Have I had anyone fitting that description? Have I buggery. One guy said, 'I didn't think it mattered.' Well, of course it matters, or I wouldn't have put it, I said.

Pause.

I also want someone who has got the gift of the gab. This is where Ben fell short again. Hardly one of the great speakers. Well actually, it's hard to come with anything that he was good at. Don't know what I saw in him in the first place. Perhaps I was just lonely.

Pause.

Anyway, I am starting a new job in the morning and I am hoping that I can meet someone there. I figure that anyone who works in a call centre must be outgoing. Hence my application for the job. I've been working for an accounting firm. I thought I could meet an accountant, a professional person. Someone suave and sophisticated. I realised after a few weeks, and after meeting all the eligible male accountants, that I would have died of boredom if I was married to one of them. Anyone who wears a blue pin-striped suit for work and spends their days looking at spreadsheets is not going to suddenly turn into Sylvester Stallone when you get him home. Trust me on that one girls.

Pause.

Don't get me wrong, not everyone who works with numbers is a nerd. I'm a bit of a number cruncher myself. This was another contentious issue with Ben. We always watched *Countdown* on Channel 4. I always got the maths equation before Ben had even got out of the blocks. I have a head for figures. Ben had difficulty dealing with being beaten all the time. It was a bit of a man thing, I think. Hurt his ego.

Pause.

The job I am starting at the call centre is number crunching. I won't be selling anything. The call centre staff will be the port of contact with the public. They'll be selling the company's products. When they have persuaded members of the public into buying our products, they will then pass them onto me and I will process the sale. It all sounds very exciting.

Pause.

Well, I must retire to bed now. I need my beauty sleep for tomorrow. It's an early start for me and I want to look my best. First impressions and all that. (*She gets up and walks to the door.*)

Fades.

Scene 2

Lights up.

Kim sits alone in the staff canteen. She is dressed smartly in business attire. The clock on wall shows 5.30 p.m.

Well I've just finished my first fortnight and it's been very eventful. I have caught the attention of one of the salespeople, Jed. He ticks all the boxes as regards boyfriend material. He is tall, handsome, good physique (obviously works out), very important and he has the gift of the gab. Just one problem, he has a wife.

Pause.

He knows that I like him. It's not something that you can hide. We've been flirting a bit, sometimes on the phone, when he passes a customer through and sometimes in person. He just seems to appear wherever I am.

Pause.

Anyway the other day he asked me to go for coffee with him after work. I agreed. I thought what harm can it do. It's only a coffee. Anyway, he breaks the ice when we meet. He tells me that he finds me very attractive and that he really enjoys being with me and would like to see more of me.

Pause.

And what of your wife? I said. He responded, 'The marriage is as good as over.' Marjorie told me only last week that she wants a divorce, and I have agreed. We sleep in separate beds.'

Pause.

Anyway, I agreed to meet up with him. We've seen each other a couple of times and texted each other. Nothing else has happened. I might be an Essex girl, but I'm not a back seat of the car sort of girl. And I haven't asked him round to my place, because of neighbours, they're particularly nosey round here. Especially Mrs Harris at number 11. She doesn't miss a trick. She could smell a married man from half a mile away, that one.

Pause.

And of course, I'm not going round to his. Marriage on the rocks or no marriage on the rocks, it isn't going to happen.

Pause.

Anyway, we were talking about the situation and he came up with an idea. He suggested that we go to a hotel in the Cotswold, which he knows. He said, 'We needed to get to know each other better.' I agreed and we just hugged in the car. 'We'll book it at work,' he said.

Pause.

I was a bit hesitant at that. Being at work and all that. But it just made more sense. I'm sure that one phone call won't hurt anyone. The office supervisor, Jill has her lunch from 12.30 to 1.30 every day. She's a real creature of habit.

Pause.

Anyway, the next day Jed came into my office with the hotel details. He rang from my phone, booked it and paid for it on his card. All done in about a minute. I feel so excited. We're going next weekend.

Pause.

Jed's told Marjorie and apparently, she's not kicking up a fuss. I don't really think I am breaking up a marriage, as the marriage was already breaking up when we met. There are no children involved. So what's the problem?

Fades.

Scene 3

Lights up.

Kim sits at home at the kitchen table. The clock on the wall shows Tuesday, 10.30 a.m.

Well, I expect you are wondering how the weekend went. And possibly wondering why on a workday, I am not at work.

Pause.

The answer is simple, I've rung in sick. I am feeling extremely low.

Pause.

The weekend went beautifully as far as I was concerned, except for the journey home.

Pause.

Everything went as planned. Jed picked me up at my flat first thing in the morning. We drove to the Cotswold and the hotel arriving just after 10.30 a.m. No sooner had we unpacked, than we were in bed making a racket. Neither of us could wait. There was some right bedroom gymnastics going on until the Monday morning when it was time to leave. We both had Monday off as it was a bank holiday. The timing of the trip couldn't have been better.

Pause.

Jed had been so attentive all weekend. A real gentleman. Opening doors for me and just generally being nice. Always asking me what I thought of my meal, when we were eating out. It was all just fantastic.

Pause.

But he just changed when we were driving back. He seemed to be in a real mood. He would not tell me why. He was just in a mood all the way back. He said that his Sat Nav wasn't working and that I should navigate. I agreed to do this, but I had told him before we set off to the hotel, that I was no good at reading maps.

Pause.

Anyway, he insisted, very firmly actually, that I navigate the way home. This situation unfortunately caused the most almighty row. Me and Ben had had some rows, but nothing like this. I was reading the map and he just kept going on about finding this road and that road. He decided to go a different way home, for reasons known only to himself.

Pause.

Anyway, we took a wrong turning and ended up heading in the wrong direction. Well, you'd think I'd accidentally pressed the nuclear button and caused World War Three with Russia. He went berserk. And in his rant, he called me something that even Ben didn't ever call me: 'A dizzy blonde.'

Pause.

I just froze when he called me that. I was unable to respond. We spent the remainder of the journey in silence. He never even looked at me. He just pulled up outside of my flat, got out of the car, unloaded my luggage and drove off without a word.

Pause.

I have not been able to contact him as his mobile is switched off. I have not gone to work today and have rung in sick. I spoke to Jill when I rang in. She seemed very sympathetic, which surprised me. I had her down as a bit of a hard faced so and so. Anyway, she informed me to take a couple of days off until I feel a lot better and then to go and see her.

Pause

The way I feel at the moment, if she sacks me it will be a relief. At least I won't have to see Jed.

Fades.

Scene 4

Lights up.

Kim sits alone again in the staff canteen. The clock shows 10.30 a.m.

Well, that was enlightening. I've just had my meeting with Jill, which I thought was going to be a return to work meeting. Which it was, with a little bit of information added onto the end. I've had to come and get a coffee to calm me down.

Pause.

The bastard's a serial cheater. He's done it before. He tries it on with every bit of 'totty' that starts here. Jill advised me to go and see Amanda in accounts.

Pause.

So off I trots to the accounts office and there is a solitary figure in the office. A blonde woman of about my age. I said to her, are you Amanda? She smiled and nodded. What happened next just blew me away. She said, 'I expect you've come to see me about Jed.' Well, yes I have as a matter of fact, I said. Jill suggested that I come and see you.

Pause.

The two of us just sat and talked. I ended up running to the toilet upset. Hence the need for a coffee. 'He's always up to it, is Jed.' She said, 'I feel so guilty that I wasn't able to warn you.' She added. The poor girl was nearly crying herself. Apparently, he'd done the same to her when she started. Showered her with praise and charmed his way around her until she gave in.

Pause.

She even told me the hotel where we stayed; because it was the same one he took her to. 'Did he tell you his marriage was on the rocks, and that they were getting divorced?' she asked. Yes, I replied. 'All lies,' she said. 'The marriage is as strong as ever. Marjorie accepts that he has a wondering eye, and even accepts him spending the weekend with another woman. On one condition – he dumps her the day after.'

Pause.

She said, 'Did he start an argument when you were travelling home?' I said yes, and it was very unpleasant. He called me a very nasty name, just for missing a turn off. She said, 'Well he insulted me for spending too long in the toilet on the way back, after a call at a service station. I was a stupid bitch.'

Pause.

I was just speechless. And then she said, that he was now hanging around the new girl who's just started in H.R.

Pause.

It was all just too much to take in. How could someone be so callus? And how could one woman inflict such misery on another, just to keep her own marriage afloat?

Pause.

I don't know whether to go and see the girl in H.R. and forewarn her.

Pause.

I am so upset, that I think I am just going to go home and have a glass of wine or two and listen to some music, and generally have some 'me' time.

Fades.

Scene 5

Kim sits alone in the lounge of her flat. She is dressed in her night attire. The clock shows midnight.

Well it's nearly time for bed. I stayed at work for the full shift. I wasn't going to let him affect my work. I had to deal with him when he put a customer through. We didn't share any banter as we generally do.

Pause.

I came home and got straight into my night attire. Intending to have an early night. I opened the bottle of wine that had been in the cooler for some time; and sat and listened to music and just chilled really.

Pause.

Then at about 7.30 p.m. the phone rang. Not my mobile but the landline. My heart was pounding because I thought it must be him. He always rang at around that time. I just sat there wondering whether to answer it or not. Then I thought, why not? If it is him, I can always tell him what a creep he is.

Pause.

I picked up the phone and said, hello. A male said, 'Hello, this is the BT engineer here, there is something wrong with your router and we need to fix it.' I remember, only last week the police pushing through a leaflet telling people to be on their guard for bogus callers, pretending to be from BT. However, in my present emotional state, all common sense went out of the window. The leaflet had said that if it is a bogus call they will not know your name. And indeed he did not, he kept referring to me as Mad-am. The leaflet explained that there had been a spate of such bogus calls in the area, and some people had fallen for it and given over their bank details and had their accounts wiped clean.

Pause.

Before I knew what I was doing I was logged onto my computer, being talked through a series of procedures. Whether it was the drink or my emotional state, I don't know. But I just did as I was told.

Pause.

And then the caller said, 'And if you just give me your bank card details madam. I will make sure that your computer is well protected.' With everything that had happened to me in the last few days. I was so confused. Maybe my brain just wasn't func-tioning properly. I ended up giving Jed's card details that had stuck in my head when he sat on my desk and booked the hotel.

Pause.

Oh well, that's what happens when you're a 'dizzy blonde.'

She gets up and walks towards the door.

Fades.

Into the garden of Eden

Sean is 40 years old and lives with his partner Julie. He has never been married, but she is divorced. They have lived together for just over a year. Sean moved into Julie's house when her divorce settlement became final. Sean works as an administrator at a local college. He is the only male in the office.

Setting

Scene 1 , 2 and 3: Wooden chair

Performance time:

10 minutes

Scene 1

Lights up.
Sean sits alone in his garden shed, which he refers to as his 'man shed'.

I blame Monty Don myself. There I was enjoying myself on a weekend just like every male on this planet, watching the footie and drinking a few lagers. Just chilling out until Monday came along. But no it couldn't last, could it? Because along comes Monty Don with his programme, *Love Your Garden*. I gets home on Friday evening a couple of weeks ago and there on the patio are more garden tools and implements than I have ever seen before in my life.

Pause.

I just stood there speechless. Then Julie came out of the house and said, 'It's no good just looking at them. You'll be using them starting tomorrow. I am sick of the garden looking like Dr Livingstone is about to appear.' I think that's a bit of an exaggeration, I said. 'I don't,' she responded. 'I want this garden immaculate just like Monty's on the television. I want a rockery, a lawn and a pond. And that's only for starters,' she added.

Pause.

I've learnt in the past that resistance is futile with Julie. Once she's set her mind on something, that's it. Apparently, that's what caused problems with her ex, Paul. He used to say: 'Julie gets what Julie wants.' Well I'm a bit more understanding than her ex, I try to give her what she wants. I'm not the most practical of guys mind. But I'll give it a go. Anything for a peaceful life. And anyway, I got this fantastic 'man shed' out of it.

Pause.

I might have lost my weekend of footie, but I've gained a place of solitude. Somewhere where I can just chill out. In between working the garden obviously. I've got plans, for the garden. I'm sure that I can make a success of this. I've already started on the vegetable patch, with a composter adjacent. There was a little problem with the composter. Julie said before she was going out for the day, 'Make sure you check on the Internet the correct dimensions.' Well, I forgot didn't I? She came back, took one look at my composter, which I might add took me all day to make, and said, 'I can tell by looking at it the slats are too wide. It won't do its job.' And blow me if she doesn't come marching out of the house with a tablet with the Internet page entitled: How to make a composter. She also had a tape measure and proceeded to measure the slats. She said, 'Just as I thought, too wide. You will have to start all over again.'

Pause.

All this took place last Sunday. Anyway, by the time I had finished it was late into the evening. And to make matters worse, I injured my hand with a hammer. I had to go to work the next day with my hand bandaged up. Not the best thing really when you spend so much time on a computer as I do. But I managed. The girls in the office thought it was amusing anyway. 'Have you been in a fight?' said Laura, who works at the next desk. (*He laughs.*) If nothing else, this gardening lark certainly gets you female attention.

Pause.

I think it was Laura who changed my name on the tea and coffee list on the wall from Sean to Monty. She's got a sense of humour that one.

Pause.

(*He gets up out of his chair.*) Well, I can't stay here all day, there's work to be done. I have a pond to dig and a rockery to create. Thank you Monty.

Fades.

Scene 2

Lights up.

Sean sits in the work staff room. He has some facial cuts and bruises.

Well it's Monday again. I'm glad to be back at work. I must be the only one in the office pleased that it's Monday. I've been working that hard in the garden; I come to work for a rest. Of course all the girls in the office think it's hilarious that I'm injured again from the weekend in the garden.

Pause.

I got back home last Friday to be told that the project for the weekend was crazy paving. Julie was waiting outside on the decking and there in piles were about 30 slabs of pavers. 'I want these all positioned near the pond,' she said. 'Use your imagination,' she said as she walked away. There goes another weekend I said under my breath.

Pause.

Anyway, I gets to work first thing on Saturday, it's boiling hot and there I am on my hands and knees positioning crazy paving. There was sweat pouring off me. All I could think about was the prisoners in the chain gangs breaking rocks. The lyrics from Sam Cooke's song: *Working in a Chain Gang* were going through my head. I thought at least the prisoners had each other for company whilst they toiled away. Here I am grafting away on my own. Occasionally Julie would come out to inspect the job.

Pause.

Anyway, the result of all the hard work over the weekend was a bad back from all the bending, and swollen fingers from manoeuvring the pavers into place. I always seemed to trap my fingers. It's a very tricky job. I was telling Laura about it at break time and she agreed to do all of the computer work, whilst I did other clerical duties. She's a diamond is Laura. An absolute diamond.

Pause.

But all this work is really worth it. The garden's looking splendid. I've just created a pond with a rockery around the side. Unfortunately, I managed to have a mishap when I filled it with water, I slipped from the side of the pond and ended up in the drink, as they say. It's hazardous this garden lark. Still, it's a talking point for the girls in the office. I often see them in little groups talking and looking my way. I bet they'll be going home and getting their hubby or partners into the garden. Well, why should they have their weekends free? A bit of male solidarity, that's what I'm looking for.

Pause.

Julie must like what I do as she is always buying me more tools and equipment. She always wants something else planting or creating. I get my orders, sorry requests, when I get home on a Friday evening.

Pause.

I've even managed to face my fear of heights through doing the garden. There's always been a big lime tree in the garden, anyway, Julie wanted it pruning and it was down as one of my jobs. She had bought me a pair of ladders for the job. With a little persuading, I managed to climb up the ladder and then onto the branches, and all whilst carrying a saw to cut the branches back. I was okay as long as I didn't look down. When I was up there all I could hear was Julie shouting words of encouragement. Anyway, job done. Cut it right back, no need to get a tree surgeon, when you can do it yourself. When I got down I had a few minor cuts to my head caused by hitting the bonce on a few branches as I was moving around from one branch to another. Hazards of the job.

Pause.

Even with all my cuts and bruises and bad back, I can still do my job in the office. Okay, some of the students give me a bit of a look when they see me with a black eye. They're probably thinking I play rugby on a weekend. They're not to know any better. It's not a problem.

Pause.

I just feel a little tired sometimes working seven days a week. But the up side of it is a lovely garden.

Pause.

And who wouldn't want that? And yes, I can put up with the banter from the girls in the office, Monty and all that. It's all good humour. There's no malice.

Pause.

I just wish I could watch the footie and have a few beers like I use to. Maybe when it's all finished I'll be able to relax again.

Pause.

Julie's going to love the end result, I'm sure.

Fades.

Scene 3

Lights up.
Sean sits alone in a bedsit. He sits on a wooden chair.

I guess you're wondering what I'm doing in this abode. What's happened to the gardening? I hear you ask. Here I am on a weekend sitting in a bedsit on my own. No Julie, giving me my jobs for the weekend.

Pause.

Events day boy. Events. As the saying goes. I went to work on the Monday of this week, on time as usual. When I walked into the office I got a really strange look from Laura and the rest of the women in the office. Then Brenda, the office manager said, 'Sean, you have a visitor in my office, I would like you to go and see her.'

Pause.

I walked into the office and there sat in the room was a young woman I have never seen before. What I didn't know when I saw her was that she was about to change my life. She smiled at me and said, 'I am Shelia from Welfare Support. I have come to see you as regards some areas of concern.' I thought I was in trouble, I immediately thought that Laura had complained about me not pulling my weight. I stuttered, what kind of concerns? I've been doing this job for a number of years and am very good at it. 'You haven't done anything wrong Sean,' she said. 'Your colleagues think very highly of you, they have just raised concerns about your injuries that you seem to have every time you come to work on a Monday.'

Pause.

Like any bloke in a similar situation I became defensive. I explained about the gardening chores and how hard I was finding it, basically working seven days a week and not getting any younger. Anyway, it wasn't long before I cracked. I just broke down. I told her everything, I blurted out, the accidents that I am having are not really accidents. I have been giving at best half-truths. 'In your own time tell me what actually happened,' she said.

Pause.

I said, the incident when I came to work with a damaged hand, I did genuinely hit my hand with a hammer like I said. But that wasn't the full story. Because I had done the composter wrong in the first place, Julie in a fit of rage stormed off and locked me out of the house. She shouted out of the kitchen window that she would not allow me back into the house until I had completed the job. The problem was the night was drawing in. And before long I was working in the pitch black. And when I was nailing the slats into place, because I could not see properly, I hit my hand.

Pause.

And when I fell into the pond, it was because I was pushed from behind. We had had words about the depth of the pond. She did not feel that I had dug it deep enough. As I turned my back on her to carry on arranging the rocks around the side, she pushed me with her foot. I fell head first into the rocks and then into the pond.

Pause.

When I was told to trim the tree. I was scared. Julie called me a coward amongst other things. When I finally climbed up the ladder and into the branches, she decided to kick the ladder away leaving me stranded. I panicked and fell through the branches, which did break my fall a bit but I twisted my ankle.

Pause.

When I had to work with swollen hands from arranging the crazy paving. My hands were swollen, because Julie had come out to inspect the job as I was arranging pavers. She didn't like the way that I had arranged them and said, 'I thought it was asking too much for you to use your imagination. The pavers are uneven.' She then walked on the one paver that I had my fingers under-neath.

Pause.

I knew as I was relaying all that went on that I could never go back. Shelia asked me a simple question: 'Why did you keep going back?' My answer was a simple one. I thought that if I made the garden what she wanted that she would feel differ-ently towards me. I thought how wonderful it would be to have a lovely garden and in the summer, to be able to sit out, just the two of us. The irony is, that the work on the garden made her even more hostile towards me. We had had some difficulties in the year we had been together and I had seen her lose her temper, but this was different. I was getting assaulted.

Pause.

It came out in the meeting that it was Laura who had raised the alarm. We agreed at the end of the meeting that I could not go home. Sheila spoke to the Council on my behalf and they found me this room in a shared house with other guys who have gone through what I have. When I think of the lyrics of *Working in a Chain Gang*, I think that in some way, I was also a prisoner. An emotional prisoner, but now I have removed the emotional chains that kept me going back.

Pause.

It's like a weight off my shoulders. I have my weekends back. And me and two of the other blokes are going to do what blokes do on a weekend – watch footie. We're going to the local pub, to sink a few pints and watch the live match.

Pause.

I'm with blokes just like me. A bit of solidarity and all that. We're the one in six blokes who have suffered domestic abuse. But not anymore. Anyway, I've got a match to watch.

Oh the bliss!

He gets up and heads towards the door.

Fades.

Three bags full

Ian Potter is in his early 30s and a newly promoted manager at a council run leisure centre in the North of England. He is married to Cathy. Ian is very ambitious and after working for the council as a supervisor at the Woolford Leisure Centre for five years, he finally got his opportunity to move into management when a senior officer, Jim Turner, spotted his potential.

Setting

Scene 1: Leisure Centre office, desk with name plate and chair

Scene 2: Armchair

Scene 3: Bar stool

Scene 4: Stool and clock

Performance time:

15 minutes

Scene 1

Lights up.

Ian sits alone in his office at the leisure centre. He sits behind a desk. At the front of the desk is a name plate: Mr Potter, Leisure Manager.

Well, all that work finally paid off. Here I am, manager of the same leisure centre where I started as a wet behind the ears leisure attendant some 15 years ago. It took me 10 years to get promoted to supervisor and then five years to get into management. Well here I am world, I've arrived. (*He points to the name plate.*) That's me Mr Potter, the manager.

Pause.

I was getting really frustrated in my career until a new senior officer came into the service, Jim Turner is his name. Ex S.A.S. Likes everything ship shape if you see what I mean. He was coming into the centre and talking to the then manager Ray Radford who was retiring, they were golf buddies. Anyway to cut a long story short my name was put in the frame for the job when Ray retired. Jim took me to one side and told me to apply. So, I did and here I am.

Pause.

There were five other candidates for the post, three from outside the Council. Anyway, they were wasting their time. I already had my foot in the door. When I went home and told Cathy I was successful she was ecstatic. You know how women get. Anyway for my first day as a manager she got me a surprise. When I went down for breakfast, on the table was a briefcase and inside was a new biro, in a fancy case. (*He holds up his new pen.*) This is no ordinary pen, it's a manager's pen.

Pause.

I'm responsible for everything in the centre. And as you would expect with that sort of responsibility comes the rewards. The paying public can't expect to get someone like me for peanuts. As well as my modest salary I have given myself some little perks. I decided that I should have my own personal car parking bay. And I wanted one that was as near to the centre as possible, so I don't have to walk through the car park to get into the building. Well the only one that I could take, was one of the disabled bays, as they are adjacent to the front of the building. I paid out of the leisure centre budget to have the bay marked: 'Managers Parking Only,' and the words 'Disabled Bay' removed. Well you should have heard the commotion from the disabled customers. Four of them were waiting for me when I pulled up for work the other day. One of them said, 'You have taken away a facility from a disabled customer.' I responded, how many of you are complaining? 'Four of us,' came the reply. And how many bays are you left with? I said. 'We had six and now we only have five,' came the reply. 'Well you have one spare then don't you,' I said, and walked off to do my job. It's tough at the top.

Pause.

I get paid by the residents of the city to make decisions, and make decisions I do. With my trusty pen I decide what needs to be done, then I do it. I model myself on Jim Turner. He's a no nonsense kind of a guy and so am I. Whenever I am faced with an issue I ask myself: What would Jim do in this situation? And the answer to resolve the matter comes straight away.

Pause.

Anyway Jim has just been into the centre and came to see me in my office. He is in the last year of a management degree and requires my help. Part of the degree requires him to implement a staff training programme. He told me from the off that the manual staff are too thick to understand anything that doesn't involve sticking their head down a toilet or mopping up a floor. He said that he will do all the paperwork stating what training has been done and if I sign it as the manager, the work can be submitted. I agreed. It sort of cuts out the middle man. Jim said that he was looking to get me on a management training course in the next year or two. Can't wait. Me and my trusty pen are going to be very busy.

Pause.

Not that I'm not busy now. I've just re-written the new programme of events for the Autumn. Made a few adjustments. Tried to make It a bit more balanced. Hasn't pleased everyone. Some people just don't like change. I decided to move the ladies keep-fit class from 1.30 – 2.30 to 3.00 – 4.00 to accommodate some of Jim's friends who wanted to use the hall for badminton and could only make 1.30. I turned up for work last Tuesday when the programme change was announced and well, what a commotion ensued. I ended up with the Mums' brigade hammering on my door. 'We can't make the latter session,' shouted the spokesperson. 'We have to pick up our kids from school at 3.00 p.m. 1.30 was just fine for us.' I explained that the programme needed more balance, blah, blah, blah. These people honestly. Where do they get off? I ask myself.

Pause.

Anyway, I must dash. I have invited Jim and his wife Tanya for dinner tonight. Cathy is cooking a lovely salmon bake. This is a sort of thank you to Jim for recognising my potential and giving me a chance to show what I can do. It'll also be a meeting of minds. One manager to another.

Fades.

Scene 2

Lights up.

Ian sits alone in an armchair in the living room of his home.

Well, that seems to have gone well. Jim and his wife, Tanya had a good time I'm sure. Me and Jim had a good chin wag and left the girls to chat in the kitchen after the meal. Jim told me that he sees me as real management potential and said that he is going to find a suitable management course for me to attend next year and he is going to take me to some management events that he attends so that I can get a feel for what lies ahead. He plays golf on a Saturday and he suggested that I attend and caddy for him so that we can discuss the next steps in my management career. Well I agreed straight away. I need the exercise and showing willingness is important to Jim. I know this. I can tell what he is thinking.

Pause.

My career is really taking off. The others at leisure centre just don't get it. They're stuck in a rut and see me climbing the ladder and they just can't seem to accept it. So, they take their frustration out on me. Take the other day for instance. Jim was running late and called in at the centre so I could sign some more of his coursework before he went to another meeting. His car was in a bit of a state because the roads were muddy. He told me that he needed the car cleaning as he could not attend a management meeting at the Guildhall and leave his dirty car in the car park looking like it had been driven through a field. He passed me the car keys and said, 'deal with it Ian, whilst I go in the gym.' So I approached one of my staff, young Leon, an attendant and told him to give Jim's car a good clean. Off he went to the cleaning cupboard to get the implements required. Next thing I had the Shop Steward marching into my office shouting about terms and conditions and this not being a job as detailed in an attendant's job description.

Pause.

I quickly went to the cupboard myself and got the sponge and a bucket of water with detergent and got cracking. As I was cleaning the car I happened to look up and I could see most of the staff in the staff room all pointing and laughing. Well we'll see who has the last laugh won't we. When they're still cleaning changing rooms I'll be sitting in the Guildhall with Jim making strategic decisions.

Pause.

The problem with people like we have at the Centre is they have no ambition and they have no respect for people like me and Jim who have a lot of responsibility. I think Jim's description of them, as thick, is a most accurate description actually. I was always taught to respect my 'betters and elders' as my mother would say. Well, if Jim is a senior manager and I am his understudy, then I have to show him due respect. And of course, as well as being a senior manager he was also in the S.A.S. He has told me some of the top secret missions that he has been on. And of course, as they are top secret, he can't tell every Tom, Dick and Harry or they wouldn't be top secret. Would they?

Pause.

Jim confides in me a lot. He knows he can trust me. He has informed me that he is looking at the leisure model, that's management talk for how the leisure centres operate in the city; and he is looking at the French model and is thinking of switching to a more continental structure. He only wants me to spearhead the change. He's probably impressed by the way I have changed the Centre's Autumn programme and thinks that I can do a similar thing across the city. He is going to France very soon on a fact finding mission and asked me tonight to join him.

Pause.

I am just so pleased that I invited Jim and his charming wife for dinner. My career is taking off like a rocket on a launch pad. I'm over the moon, if you pardon the pun. Over the moon. I'll be taking my trusty pen with me, it's my constant companion.

Fades.

Scene 3

Lights up.

Ian sits alone in the bar of a French Hotel. He sips a glass of wine. He is dressed in casual attire.

Well, what a working holiday this is. (*He smiles as he sips the wine.*) Jim has given me the night off. Jim met with all his French counterparts today on the golf course. I caddied for him. It all got a little too much for my body. My muscles ached, carrying a bag of heavy golf clubs takes its toll in the end. Jim told me to go and get the masseur from the hotel to give my back and shoulders the 'once over', as he put it. 'Put it on the expenses,' he said. So I have.

Pause.

Jim trusts me implacably. He has only put me in charge of everything. I knew the pen would come in handy. I arranged the hotel. All Jim said was he wanted to stay in a good quality one, preferably one near the golf course. So he didn't have far to travel to meet the French contingent. So I used my management skills and picked this one. It's a 4 star hotel. Anyway, as Jim has put me in charge of expenses the hotel management deal with me. I sign all the expenses sheets with my trusty pen. Jim leaves the completed forms at the reception for any activities that he has done, then after breakfast I am presented with the forms and I sign them. No problem.

Pause.

Jim has hired a car tonight to entertain one of the French senior managers. Attractive young woman she is. She is taking him to one of the leisure centres with a hotel complex. Jim said that he wants to see first-hand how the dual service operates, and said that it might be a long evening because it's a long drive. And he felt that given my long day on the golf course, I should take the evening off to recover for the next day, which will be another day on the golf course. This is modern management, the golf course is where all the business of the day is discussed. Jim said that when we get back he will hand me all his notes and let me write a report for the Director of Leisure, basically Jim's boss. And he answers to senior councillors.

Pause.

You know I almost feel sorry for the morons left behind. There they are cleaning changing rooms and here I am in France organising events for Jim's fact finding trip. I left one of the supervisors in charge for the week. It was hard to pick which one to step up and fill my shoes. They are all a bit on the thick side if you get my drift. Not exactly the sharpest tool in the box. They couldn't re-arrange the Centre's programme, so it's a good job I did it before I set off. Basically, I have done all the big jobs, all they have to do is oversee the day to day operation.

Pause.

It's a real doddle here. If I am not on the golf course, I am generally in the hotel relaxing. Jim said that I should spend some time 'chilling out', as he put it. He said everything would be covered on the expenses, so if I want to have a few drinks in the bar; then I can. Well who's going to say no to that? Not me that's for sure, I've been known to sink a few pints in my time I can tell you, and if I'm not paying, then so be it. I have spent some time visiting some of the leisure centres here, but not that many. They look very much like the ones back home to be honest. But I am sure Jim knows what he is doing.

Pause.

I can't wait to get back and submit my report. It's my report that the Director of Leisure will be reading. It will state: author of report, Ian Potter.

Pause.

Yes, I can see me in the Guildhall having meetings. It won't be long now. When the fact-finding report is submitted, it'll be 'send for Mr Potter'. This man has potential. It's only a matter of time.

Pause.

Well must retire to bed. It's an early start on the golf course tomorrow morning. (*He gets up out of the chair.*)

Fades.

Scene 4

Ian sits alone in a prison cell. He sits on a wooden chair. A clock in background shows it's 3.50 p.m.

Well, I always said that I wanted to have meetings at the Guildhall. I can certainly tick that box. I had my first and only meeting there two weeks after returning home from the fact-finding trip to France. Unfortunately, it wasn't the meeting I anticipated; it was my disciplinary.

Pause.

Jim never came back from the trip. All along he was using the trip to line up a new position for himself. A career move. He told me that he would travel back the next day after me as he had important business to see to. He had already tendered his notice to the Director by email. He took his annual leave which he had saved up and left immediately.

Pause.

Of course, I was unaware of all this until everything started to unravel. And everything certainly unravelled. When I went to work on my first day back, an officer, John Francis from Human Resources was waiting for me in my office, along with a representative from the managers union that I had just joined. Francis said, 'As of this minute you are suspended from your role. You are to leave the Centre immediately.'

Pause.

Well, I was shell shocked. What about the report I am going to write, I said. 'I don't think we are interested in your report at this stage,' he said.

Pause.

As I stood in the car park with my union representative, I could see all the staff in the staff room looking out and laughing. Talk about deja vu. My representative told me that the Council had received all the expenses forms that I had signed and had alerted the police, as they felt that fraud had taken place. What about Jim? I said. He said, 'You mean the "Scarlet Pimpernel," they seek him here, they seek him there. He's gone and unlike the real Pimpernel he's not coming back from France. He's left you to face the music.' Face the music, I said never. He saw action in the Falklands with the S.A.S. He's not going to duck out of a showdown with anyone, certainly not a bunch of pen push-ers. 'Never got past the cadets,' he said. 'All a fabrication.'

Pause.

It was whilst I was on suspension for two weeks, that I learnt he had got his management degree. And that the forms I had supplied regarding the staff training were challenged, but Jim had put a statement in saying that he took the documents and their contents in good faith. He got a First. He no doubt used his degree to get his new job.

Pause.

I attended my disciplinary and was instantly dismissed for mak-ing fraudulent expenses claims and for bringing the Council into disrepute for signing training documents that I knew to be untrue. Shortly after the disciplinary I was arrested at home by the police and charged with fraud.

Pause.

On the advice of my solicitor I pleaded guilty, when it went to court. I received six months as it was my first offence. Cathy attended the hearing, but then filed for divorce. At least I didn't have to attend court for that one. It was granted as a 'quickie' divorce, as they say.

Pause.

Here I am now, with no office with my nameplate on the desk. But, residing at her majesty's pleasure in an open prison. Have to share with a guy called John who like me has been done for fraud. Only his one was on a master scale. He defrauded the Government out of thousands of pounds in benefit claims. He's from a notorious family in Manchester. Prison is home from home for him. The other prisoners call him the 'governor', because he is the boss. Which is bad news for me. I am basically his 'runner', I do little errands for him. So there's no change there then. I take little parcels to other inmates, that sort of thing.

Pause.

It's what got me in here in the first place. (*He gets up from his chair.*) I must dash, John told me that I have to be at the laundry at precisely 4 p.m. to pick up a parcel.

Fades.

Turning back the clock

Brian is 59 years old, slightly overweight with thinning hair. He has been married to Caroline for seven years. It is the second marriage for both of them. Brian divorced his first wife for adultery. As he approaches his 60th birthday he starts to think about his youth.

Setting

Scene 1: Armchair

Scene 2: Office desk and chair

Scene 3: Bench

Scene 4: Chair in bedroom

Performance time:

15 minutes

Scene 1

Lights up.

Brian sits alone in an armchair in the living room of the house he shares with Caroline.

I can't believe I am nearly 60. I've found myself thinking back a lot recently, to a time when I was younger, when I was slimmer and had hair. I would never reveal this to Caroline, but I have been thinking a lot about a girl I was seeing when I was 18. I can't seem to stop thinking about her, Michelle was her name.

Pause.

We worked together in a fashion shop in the 1970s, well to be exact it was the summer of 1976. The hottest summer on record. And it was hot for me if you see what I mean. We just hit it off, me and Michelle. We just couldn't get enough of each other. At work, at each other's houses when parents were away. Anywhere really.

Pause.

I thought it was the real thing. Head over heels I was. Hopelessly in love. I bet you're thinking, what happened then?

Pause.

Well I'll tell you. But I can't give you all the information; because I don't know myself. I turned up for work one day, dressed to the nines as you'd expect for a 'man about town' guy like me; and I was told that Michelle had left. That she would not be coming back and had left the area.

Pause.

Well, I was gob smacked, but not as gob smacked as I was the other day. I only saw her, Michelle. I was on the bus going into town. When I looked out of the window, there was Michelle just coming out of a shop. She looked gorgeous. Just like she used to look, only a bit older. It was definitely her. I got off at the next stop and ran back, but she'd gone.

Pause.

There I was puffing and panting after just running a few yards. I used to be as fit as a fiddle. Put on a few pounds since then. I looked at myself in a shop window and all I could see was a fat belly. I thought it's a good job I didn't see Michelle looking like this.

Pause.

This close encounter was the impetus I needed to join a gym. I found a gym in the town centre and signed on the bottom line, and then went to the nearest sports shop and got kitted out. Can't wait to get started.

Pause.

I told Caroline when I got home. About the gym that is, not about the close encounter with an old flame. I'm not that stupid.

Pause.

Anyway, I just got a look that only a woman can give, when she saw the sports equipment. She probably thinks I going through a mid-life crisis.

Pause.

Mind, she's been acting a bit strangely herself. Has been very secretive. Always on the computer in the study, and when I walk towards the room she hurriedly comes off the programme she was on. I know she has a Facebook account. And when her mobile rings she disappears into the next room to talk to whoever.

Pause.

It's all very strange behaviour if you ask me. My first wife, Sharon used to act like this. This is the 1980s you understand. No mobiles or social media. We just had a landline. If the phone rang and she answered, she used to close the lounge door so I couldn't hear. And if I answered the person used to hang up. I discovered later down the line, that she was speaking to her lover. A guy she met at work, and eventually cleared off with. Anyway, I have spoken to Caroline about her behaviour and she assures me everything is fine.

Pause.

I am just frightened that history will repeat itself.

Fades.

Scene 2

Lights up.

Brian sits alone in the office where he works. He is at his desk.

I've never really understood women. Which is probably why I'm on my second marriage. Never really been a talker. I'm much more of a physical person. When I was with Michelle it was great, sex was the main part of the relationship. Problem now is that as I've got older and particularly put on a few pounds, the sex is not as often as I would like.

Pause.

I'm hoping that the gym work will make a bit of a difference. I've been a bit body conscious since I put a few inches on around the waist. I've not been wanting Caroline to see me naked. Bit of a problem that in a relationship.

Pause.

Anyway, if that seems a bit of odd behaviour, Caroline is not behaving much better. Maybe we're both going through a mid-life crisis. Her with her Facebook fixation. I am certain there must be another man in this somewhere.

Pause.

It's all very odd if you ask me. It's a bit like the behaviour of my first wife, Sharon. I confided in a bloke at work about her behaviour. He told me she was probably having an affair – and he was right. She was. I challenged her, but she denied it. I found out the hard way, by coming home early from work.

Pause.

Anyway, I decided to confront Caroline about her behaviour. Are you having an affair, I said. 'No,' she said. 'But I think you need to show me more attention,' she added. Attention, it's always attention with women.

Pause.

Anyway, the gym work seems to be paying off. I've lost two inches around the waist and feel better in myself. A bit more confident in myself. After one session in the gym I even plucked up the courage to talk to a young woman who was using the cycle machine next to me. Joanne, they call her. Nice looking woman. I even thought about asking her out. Well you never know. These things happen when things aren't going well at home.

Pause.

I don't know if this is a mid-life crisis. But I've been thinking about Joanne quite a lot lately. Talking to her in the gym seemed to trigger things off. Even in the intimate moments if you see what I mean. Caroline felt frisky the other night and she made the first move in bed. Straight away I started to think about

Joanne in her tight fitting training pants. Skin tight they are. Anyway, I got that carried away I was worried in case I started yelling out her name.

Pause.

Anyway, it did the trick in the bedroom. Caroline was well satisfied with my performance. Little did she know what was going on in the head. Some things are best not out in the open. And I don't know what she thinks about whilst we are at it. Could be the bloke down the road for all I know, or the young fit guy who works in the local garage. Who knows?

Pause.

Anyway, the way she's been acting lately, it may all be academic. If she's having an affair, I'll be off. I didn't stand for it in my first marriage and I'm not standing for it now. Life's too short. I'm approaching 60 and I may need to find somebody else.

Pause.

And you never know. It may just be that Joanne likes older men, and I've lost so much weight and feel 10 years younger, I reckon I could still do the business with a younger woman.

Pause.

There's life in the old dog yet. (*He winks.*) It could be like turning the clock back to my teenage years, when me and Michelle were at it like there was no tomorrow.

Pause.

Well better get back to work. (*He gets up from the chair.*)

Fades.

Scene 3

Lights up.

Brian is dressed in his gym attire. He sits on a bench in the changing room.

Well, it's certainly been a crazy last fortnight. Basically, me and Joanne have been seeing each other, and it's getting serious.

Pause.

It all started one Saturday. I walked into the gym as normal and there was Joanne, sat on the exercise cycle. She smiled as I walked towards her. Before I knew it I was talking to her and I suggested that we meet for coffee after our workout. She agreed and when we sat down and talked, the age difference just didn't matter, nor did our commitment to other people. She told me her age which turns out she is 41 and I told her that I am nearly 60.

Pause.

So we got the age difficulty over with fairly easily. Then we started talking about our other halves. Turned out she lives with this right plonker who is my age and treats her really badly. Goes out on the booze every night and leaves her alone. Hence the gym visits. I explained to her that I am married, but I believe that my wife is having an affair. We were just so honest with each other.

Pause.

It turns out that Joanne and her partner very rarely have sex, and next thing you know me and her are at it, in my car. Not in the gym car park, you understand. I drove to a nice quiet place in the country, so we could talk more privately, and events sort of unfolded really.

Pause.

Going to the gym, meeting up and having sex in my car, in a hotel, you name it, we went there and got at it. I haven't had such great sex with someone since Michelle. It's great. But it's gone beyond the sex. I think of her all the time and she told me the same.

Pause.

Then the inevitable happened. We started to discuss the future. We knew we had to be together. I explained to her that I could not leave Caroline before my 60th birthday. I owed her that much, and there was the family to think of. My two sisters wouldn't think too highly of me if I was to walk out prior to the big day. It was only a fortnight away and I just couldn't walk out just before it. But I could just after.

Pause.

Joanne understood. She would leave her partner tomorrow if she could. However, she saw my predicament. We agreed that we would wait until the day after my birthday, and we would then both tell our other halves at the same time that we were leaving. It was agreed that I would go and stay in a hotel until Joanne's partner cleared off out of her flat.

Pause.

It was all agreed. I just want to get my birthday out of the way. I don't think that Caroline would have gone to too much trouble given that she has someone else. I'm sure it will come as a release for her. She can start afresh with this new chap. We can come to some agreement over the house, and she can keep the cat.

Pause.

These things have a habit of working out. I'm sure everything is going to be just fine. Well, I can't stay here all day, I've got my training to do and I'm meeting Joanne afterwards. (*He gets up and walks towards the changing room door.*)

Fades.

Scene 4

Lights up.

Brian sits alone in the spare bedroom of his house. He sits on a wooden chair. He looks tired as if he has not slept.

Well the last fortnight or so has to be the most difficult time of my life. This room isn't a hotel room. Things didn't go to plan.

Pause.

I woke up on my birthday next to Caroline. We had a bit of a cuddle, nothing else. She wished me happy birthday and said she had a surprise for me. And off she went and got me an envelope, along with an enormous 60th birthday card. I was already starting to feel a bit anxious about the next day, I can tell you. I had booked myself into a hotel room and had told Joanne what was happening. I was going to tell Caroline first thing in the morning, after my birthday that I was leaving. I figured I could be packed and out of there within an hour or so.

Pause.

Anyway, I nervously opened the card and it was a romantic card with a lovely message inside telling me how much she loved me. Oh shit, I thought. Have I miss-read the messages? Then I opened the envelope, inside were two tickets for Hull City versus Sunderland for later in the afternoon. My birthday fell on a

Saturday. Caroline is from Sunderland and I'm from Hull. She said: 'When we first met you took me for our first date to watch Hull City versus Sunderland. And I want you to take me again. You are the only one I want to watch football with.' I was speechless.

Pause.

We set off for the game at about 1.30. I really didn't enjoy it one little bit. Sunderland won one nil and I couldn't have cared less. It was a slow journey home. I couldn't stop thinking of the next day and what I was going to do.

Pause.

Then we turned into the street and there were cars everywhere. 'I've invited a few people round for drinks to celebrate,' she said. And out of the house came my two sisters and everyone in the family. Caroline kissed me on the cheek and said, 'Happy birthday darling.' I just froze.

Pause.

Then we got into the house and worse was to come. Everyone was around me patting me on the back and wishing me well. Music from the 1970s was blearing out. Then Caroline said, 'Not everyone attending your birthday is present in the room. There is a special guest. Waiting in the living room for you.' Caroline continued. 'You might have wondered why I have been on Facebook and my mobile recently. Well, I tracked down one of you old work colleagues. You told me about her when we first met. So I wanted to track her down to attend your special day.' And out of the living room came Michelle. Oh my God I thought. She looked stunning. And then Caroline said, 'And she has brought her daughter with her, Joanne.' Oh my God. I looked at Joanne, and she at me, then Michelle looked at me and then Joanne. Then Caroline looked at me and then the other two.

Pause.

No man should ever go through what I've just been through. I have been so distraught, that I can't even sleep in the same bed as Caroline. I've had to take the spare bed.

Pause.

If only I hadn't thought that history was repeating itself, I wouldn't have gone to the gym. I wouldn't have had an affair. I daren't even contemplate what I might have actually done, given Joanne's age. Born just after Michelle left the shop. I couldn't even ask Michelle, why she left so suddenly. Mother and daughter have gone now. But what of me and Caroline? Who knows? Time's a healer as they say. And as my mother used to say, 'Let sleeping dogs lie.'

Fades.

d-product-compliance